Still Life With Children

Still Life With Children

Selected Poems of Francesc Parcerisas
translated from the Catalan by Cyrus Cassells

STEPHEN F. AUSTIN STATE UNIVERSITY PRESS

For information about permission to reproduce selections from this book, contact *Permissions*, at sfapress@sfasu.edu

For information about special discounts for bulk purchases, contact *Distribution* at sfapress@sfasu.edu or 1-936-468-1078

Production manager: Kimberly Verhines
Interior design: Sarah Johnson
Cover art and design: Margo Berdeshevsky

ISBN 978-1-62288-543-5

Stephen F. Austin State University Press
P.O. Box 13007 SFA Station
Nacogdoches, Texas 75962
sfapress@sfasu.edu
www.sfasu.edu/sfapress
936-468-1078

Contents

ACKNOWLEDGMENTS

Many thanks to the *Institut Ramon Llull* for a generous resident fellowship, which allowed me to work in Barcelona, and to Trinity University's *Journal of Literary Translation* for devoting a special issue to several of these translations; to Francesc Parcerisas for his kind, lively participation and cooperation in Barcelona, Eivissa (Ibiza), and Vilanova i La Geltrú; and to Margo Berdeshevsky for her cover art and for encouraging me to bring Parcerisas's wonderful work into English.

The following poems appeared in American, British, and Irish journals and anthologies:

Academy of American Poets Poem-A-Day: "Virgil's Hand"
Being Human (Bloodaxe Books): "Shave"
Borderlands: "Cemetery at the Chapel of Saint Eulalia d'Alendo,"
"Altarpiece at 'The Cloisters"
The Cimarron Review: "Sunset"
"Empty Apartment Building in Summer"
Connotations Press: Congeries: "The Good Thief"
"Old Tree, II"
The Cortland Review: "Snowy Cemetery"
"To Keep Watch Over the Language"
Counterfeits: World Literature in Translation: "December Orange"
The Ecco Anthology of International Poetry: "Act of Gratitude"
The Enchanting Verses Literary Review: "Sibyl"
In The Shape of a Human Body I am Visiting the Earth (McSweeneys):
"Act of Gratitude"
JOLT (The Journal of Literary Translation, Trinity College): "Cellar"
"Clear Night"
"The Emperor Hadrian Muses on the Golden Age"
"Imagining My Son, Seated in a Corner of this Eatery in Fifty Years"
"Portrait of the Poet"
"Rain"
"The Shadow"

Nine Mile:	"Mud Pie"
	"Vienna, Christmas 1939"
	"Taxidermist"
The Literati Quarterly:	"Matchbox"
	"The Sin-Eater"
The New Works Review:	"Germany: The End of World War II"
Poetarium:	"Objects"
Poetry International:	"Act of Gratitude"
	"After Anne Sexton"
	"Holy Week"
	"Severed Hand"
	"Shave"
	"Then"
Taos Journal of International Poetry and Art:	"Calypso"
	"The Orchard"
	"Dogs"
Two Lines:	"December Orange"
Center for the Art of Translation website:	"The Egyptian Museum"
Words Without Borders:	"Then"
	"Shave"

Poems in this volume are from *L'edat d'or* (*The Golden Age*), 1983; *Focs d'octubre* (*October Fires*), 1991; *Natura morta amb nens* (*Still Life with Children*), 2000; *Dos dies més de sud* (*Two More Days in the South*), 2006; and *Seixanta-un poemes* (*Sixty-One Poems*), 2014 from *The Golden Age*:

"Calypso"
"Dogs"
"The Emperor Hadrian Muses on the Golden Age"
"Shave"
"Rain"
"Virgil's Hand"
"Portrait of the Poet"

from *October Fires*:

"Altarpiece at 'The Cloisters'"
"Clear Night"
"The Egyptian Room"
"Sibyl"
"Sunset"
"Taxidermist"

from *Still Life with Children*:

"After Anne Sexton"
"Cellar"
"Empty Apartment Building in Summer"
"Germany: The End of World War II"
"Imagining My Son . . ."
"Match Box"
"Mud Pie"
"Objects"
"Snowy Cemetery"
"The Good Thief"
"The Sin-Eater"

from *Two More Days in the South*:

> "Act of Gratitude"
> "Cemetery at the Hermitage of Saint Eulalia d'Alendo"
> "December Orange"
> "Holy Week"
> "Old Tree, II"
> "Then"
> "The Orchard"

from *Sixty-One Poems*

> "Severed Hand"
> "The Shadow"

Introduction: Francesc Parcerisas And The Timeless Mediterranean

Francesc Parcerisas's concise, deftly modulated poems pledge allegiance to family, fatherhood, humor, philosophy, desire, and the abiding presence of the Mediterranean. Parcerisas's voice is relaxed, cosmopolitan, supple, and quite capable of becoming sensual, amused, or trenchant at will—a sea change from the gravity and nationalism of the embattled generation of Catalan poets that preceded him. In his wide-awake poems, small artifacts and gestures often serve as touchstones to memory; there is consistently an unforced reverence for the domestic and the quotidian in his poetry that lends ordinary events and objects—such as a marble in a boy's palm or a matchbox found in the attic—an enigmatic, restorative glow. Parcerisas is clearly a soul-sharing poet of small treasures, an ambassador of the blessings of a savored life: "Relish this tiny ecstatic moment / that enriches everything," the poet encourages the reader.

With dash and a certain degree of subversive glee, he applies modern psychology to the "gaps" in Homer's *Odyssey*: in lively conversation at his summer home, Parcerisas mentions Homer's cursory allusion to the seven years that Ulysses spends with the sea-nymph Calypso, insisting, "seven years is a long time for any relationship!" In their offhand allusiveness to the classical world, Parcerisas's poems convey the sense of a timeless Mediterranean where ancient and contemporary men and women are linked through domestic rituals and romantic foibles; in "Empty Apartment Building in Summer," the estranged, lovelorn speaker declares:

I relish the day's brilliance
and the body's,
with leftover fruit becoming
ever more fragrant as it dries—
so that in our wounding,
you won't haul me the callous way
Achilles' chariot once dragged
young Hector's broken body.

The classical allusion here and elsewhere in Parcerisas's work isn't merely highflown decoration or reflexive erudition but instead exists in stalwart service to revelation; the poet's (and speaker's) sense of reference and memory extend deep into the Mediterranean past.

Born in 1944, Francesc Parcerisas, the author of fifteen volumes of poetry, is considered the premier Catalan poet of his generation—a "miracle generation" of poets who came of age as Franco's public banning of the Catalan language came to an end. He is also a masterly, award-winning translator of an impressive array of significant international writers, including F. Scott Fitzgerald, Doris Lessing, Katherine Mansfield, Joyce Carol Oates, Cesare Pavese, Edgar Allan Poe, Ezra Pound, Rimbaud, Susan Sontag, William Styron, and Nobel Laureate Seamus Heaney, who has had a direct influence on Parcerisas's poetic strategies. Among his numerous translations from French, Italian, and English into Catalan, he is most famous in Catalonia for his translation of Tolkien's *The Lord of the Rings*.

I first met Francesc Parcerisas in Barcelona in the summer of 1983 when I came to explore Gaudi's sensual, magical city and to translate the poetry of Salvador Espriu (1913-1985), who was, at the time, the leading Catalan candidate for the Nobel Prize. I remember Francesc from that period as very energetic and affable, very generous with his time, and patient with an outsider avid to learn about Catalan literature and culture.

In 2005, I returned to Barcelona after an absence of two decades, and Francesc graciously invited me to a meal at his home. In his living room, he recited, movingly, in Catalan, the poem "Objects," which prompted an almost lightning-quick decision on my part to become his translator.

Soon after, we traveled together by train to Arenys de Mar, the Costa Maresme town where the poet Salvador Espriu spent his childhood summers and is now interred in the columbarium of the town's commanding hilltop cemetery, which dramatically overlooks the sea. I had translated Espriu's earliest volume *Sinera Cemetery* and had spent an evening with the famously reclusive, hieratic poet shortly before his death, and my long-deterred visit to the cypress-lined cemetery was, for me, the completion of an extraordinary spiritual and cultural journey.

Our pilgrimage to venerate Espriu, the grand man of Catalan letters, cemented our bond and my determination to render Parcerisas's poetry into English. Though many individual poems have been translated into English and several European languages, this is the first full selection of Parcerisas's work to be published in America.

In the fall of 2006, under the auspices of the *Institut Ramon Llull,* which promotes Catalan literature, I worked on this volume, at a research dormitory near the renowned Ramblas, the wide promenade peopled with spectacularly-costumed mimes, acrobats, musicians, and chalk-artists, making it seem a Mediterranean Oz. A lauded translator himself, Francesc Parcerisas kindly responded to my queries and encouraged me to come up with viable English versions. Overall, I opted for much shorter lines and rhythms than the original Catalan, while striving to retain meaning and nuance.

In August 2007, I had the wonderful opportunity of visiting Parcerisas on the island of Eivissa (Ibiza), where he summers in a house he built with friends forty years before, a sanctum far from the dawn-treading revelers and deejays who have transformed the island into an international playground—a compound replete with inviting hammocks, emerald lizards, and thick white Balearic walls, ideally tucked away in the hills above Sant Antoni, and graced with a panoramic view of the bay.

I was surprised to learn, during my stay at "Puig Pere Toni," (the hill of Pere Toni), that Parcerisas did not grow up speaking Catalan at home, but made the decision to compose poetry in it, partly because he associated the suppressed Catalan language with patrimony and culture, and enforced Castilian (in the aftermath of the Spanish Civil War, public signs that read "Don't bark; speak the language of the empire!" were common in defeated Barcelona) with Franco's callous, confederate reign of repression. He tells the story of being riveted by a red and yellow Catalan flag discovered inside the coffin of a relative who had died during the war—a flag that turned to dust on contact; for the young poet, the imperiled Catalan language was profoundly linked to the cornerstones of family, justice, and spiritual endurance.

In *The Odyssey,* wandering Ulysses returns home with insights gleaned from a seafaring life deeply lived, and Parcerisas likewise seems to bring to his poems an anchoring, shareable, acquired wisdom. Here are some lines from "Ithaca," a Constantine Cavafy poem, which seem very much in the spirit of Parcerisas's blessedly sane and appealing work, though, of course, Parcerisas's vivid homeplace is an Ithaca of puddle-jumping kids, rueful lovers, and idling taxicabs!

Always keep Ithaca in your mind.
To arrive there's your ultimate goal.
But don't hurry the voyage at all.
It's better to let it last for many years;
and to anchor at the island when you're old,
rich with all you've gained on the way,
not expecting Ithaca will offer you riches.

Ithaca has given you the marvelous voyage.
Without her, you would have never set out on the road.
She has nothing more to give you.

And if you find her poor, Ithaca hasn't deceived you.
Wise as you've become, so experienced,
you must already have understood what Ithacas mean.

I chose *Still Life with Children* as the title for this selected volume, because of its engaging immediacy, but also because of my strong sense of Parcerisas as a dedicated and intrepid father to his impressively multi-lingual sons, Nil and Pol, who speak Catalan, Spanish, and English with rapid-fire fluency. Parcerisas came to fatherhood later in life, and brings a still-vibrant, mature man's patience and perspective to his parenting. On a dog-day afternoon, drenched in the sound of cicadas, he sets the wine, the bread, and anchovy-filled olives on the table for his sons and me, and envisions ancient families doing the same or picnicking beside the Mediterranean, reminding me that this "still life," these timeless familial gestures and rituals are the essence of human consolation and communion.

"Puig Pere Toni," Eivissa (Ibiza), August 2007

Francesc Parcerisas and Cyrus Cassells at the grave of Salvador Espriu,
Sinera Cemetery, Arenys de Mar, 2005
Photo by Margo Berdeshevsky

Still Life with Children

AFAITAT

Contempla't al mirall, desconegut i igual,
ensopit pel son, sorprès de veure't.
Aquests solcs o aquesta grisor a les temples
ja els has anat acceptant de grat
—hoste feliç quasi imprevist—,
que no recordes quin dia va aparèixer.
És el preu descarat que et cal pagar
per la fictícia intimitat del cos.
I, ara, comença a afaitar-te.
La fulla, abans ràpida i freda,
ja no llisca, tensa, per la pell
amb frec plaent d'esquí jovenívol:
has de tibar la galta flàccida
amb els dits. No desesperis.
Potser si evites, astut per força,
la marca vergonyant d'un tall
podràs oblidar que l'aliança amb el cos
ja ha començat a dissoldre's.

SHAVE

Observe yourself in the mirror,
unchanged yet strange,
still shaggy with sleep, startled
at seeing your likeness.
These wrinkles, these graying temples
that you've already accepted gracefully
—affable guests who showed up
so suddenly, that you can't quite recall
their initial appearance,
are emblems of the shameless price required
for this fictitious intimacy with the body.
And now, begin to shave.
The blade, once quick and cold, no longer
glides taut across your skin like the pleasant
lickety-split friction of youthful skis:
you're forced to stretch your flabby cheek
with your fingers. Don't despair.
Perhaps if you're shrewd and willfully avoid
the shameful mark of a knick,
you'll forget your alliance with your body
has already begun to dissolve.

Taronja de desembre

Escolto la dolça taronja de desembre:
em diu "no,"
em diu "mai més,"
em diu "potser encara."
Només a l'hivern cauen amb aquesta força
les gotes al pati. La pluja i els morts
em desperten. Miren els passatgers
del transbordador els qui han quedat
a la platja: benvinguts, o perduts,
sense cap por, encara. Son beneïda.
Em són amables i hi compto.
Amb les mans et busco l'esquena
com si la roda no pogués mai escapçar
un cos que és jove i que delira de goig.
Per això la taronja és dolça
i ho és la llum de desembre,
i el rostre que la persiana desdibuixa
un cop més, amb la vida discreta
que ens enganya. I creix, i ens deixa.
Amb lentitud el transbordador s'allunya.
La polpa és el suc roig de tota l'alba.

December Orange

I listen to the sweet December orange:
it tells me *No*,
then *Nevermore*,
then *Maybe still.*
Only in wintertime
do plummeting raindrops on the patio
splatter with such intensity.
The tempest and the dead
jar me awake.
Look at the ferry passengers, the ones
too long at the beach:
welcome or lost, dauntless,
and still at large.
Sleep when it comes to us
is blessed;
I prize and depend on all this:
as if time's wheel wouldn't dare
savage such a young body
alive with pleasure,
I reach for your back.
The orange is also sweet,
and through it, I acquire
December's light,
and the face the Venetian blinds
blur, once more,
with their aura of a discreet,
betraying life
that burgeons and finally
abandons us.
Slowly, slowly, the ferry departs.
The pulp is the ruddy juice
of the entire dawn.

Sala egípcia

M'assec a la sala egípcia del museu
i sento el brunzir de mel de les abelles.
El passat és de debò: groc i blau,
com el blat que agrana el pagès o aquesta cigonya
que beu al riu turquesa del papir.
Un cop més tot em sembla igual:
el paleta amb el sedàs a bat de sol
i l'esclau que venta, submís, el faraó
m'esperen dins un taxi, carrer avall.
Un vol d'ànecs rabents creua el cel enterbolit;
a la taula del costat, l'ibis somica, ebri, cruel.
Diuen que les passions no es poden mai pintar
però aquest fresc és un mirall de quatre mil anys.
Vindrà la mort, com el gos fosc de la paret,
i creurem ser massa joves, o immadurs,
o ens sabrà greu de traspassar, adormits,
el goig escàs i fugisser de tants moments perduts.
La barca, però, llisca eterna sota el sol roent.

THE EGYPTIAN ROOM

Sitting in the museum's Egyptian room,
I'm an audience for
a honey-rich buzzing of bees.
The past's fully alive:
yellow and blue,
akin to the laborer's threshed wheat,
or that stork sipping
from a turquoise river
captured on papyrus.
In a flash, everything's scrambled:
the stonemason with his sieve
in the pitiless sun
and the slave meekly
fanning the pharaoh
wait for me in a taxicab
down the street.
A flock of in-a-hurry ducks
crosses the overcast sky;
an ibis snivels at the next table,
soused and barbarous.
Folks claim passions
can't be painted any longer,
but this fresco's
a four-thousand-year-old mirror.
Like the mural's black mongrel,
death will arrive,
and we'll imagine ourselves
unripe, unready,
or we'll lament having
to surrender in sleep
so many scant, fleeting
moments of joy,
well aware the Nile barge glides
endlessly under the blazing sun.

ACCIÓ DE GRÀCIES

Gràcies, àngel. Gràcies, dimonis de la nit.
Gràcies, hivern del cor on cremen
els troncs secs del desig. Gràcies,
llum del fred, nit de les aigües.
Gràcies, odi biliós de mitjanit,
llor de la matinada, puput de l'alba.
Per allò diferent, inesperat, esquerp,
pel dolor i pel mal, gràcies.
Per tot el que som i el que no som,
per allò que evitem, o que volem.
Gràcies per tu i per mi.
Per la paraula perdó, argent,
amor. Gràcies pel sí i pel no.
Per poder donar-te les gràcies
i perquè no calgui fer-ho.
Gràcies per la por, pel pa,
per l'oli, gràcies per la nit.
Gràcies per l'amor de matinada,
per la moneda que trobem al terra,
per l'aigua de la font,
per la teva mà damunt la galta.
Gràcies pels teus ulls i pels teus llavis,
gràcies per cridar amb joia el meu nom.
Gràcies, mort, perquè existeixes
i fas que allò que és
sigui ara tan viu endins de mi,
i sigui bell, ple, rodó, teu.

ACT OF GRATITUDE

Thank you, angel. Thank you,
demons of the night.
Thank you, winter,
season in which the heart burns
arid tree-trunks of desire. Thank you,
bracing cold light, nocturnal water.
Thank you, midnight bile,
laurel of morning, hoopoe of dawn.
For what's odd, unexpected, wild,
for evil and pain, thank you.
For the sum of what we are
and are not,
for all we avoid
and all we crave.
Thanks for the lush words,
love and silver,
for yourself and myself.
Thank you for yes and for no.
For the ability to give thanks
and for rendering them unnecessary.
Thanks for fear,
for bread and oil,
for the night time.
Thank you for lovemaking
at the break of day, for the coin
discovered on the ground,
for your hand on my cheek,
the gush of the fountain.
Thank you for your eyes and lips,
for crying out my name
with joy.

Many thanks, death,
for your existence,
for making all these things
more vivid inside me—
so very yours,
so beautiful, brimming, and complete.

PIS BUIT A L'ESTIU

L'escala és silenciosa al brogit esquerdat de l'ascensor.
Tothom és fora. El carrer sembla mig buit.
Un tomàquet menut a la nevera és una postal
del desig que ens enarbora. Mira com compartim
no res: mitja fulla d'enciam i el teló de llum
que ens eclipsa el futur. Vindran dies inútils,
l'ombra del desengany, la melangia,
el torment dolç o amarg com una ratlla feta a terra.
El teu cabell fa olor de pintura,
les meves mans d'adéus inútils.
Guardo la resplendor del dia i la del cos
amb la fruita que s'asseca, olorosa
—que el dolor no me l'arrossegui, cruel,
com el carro d'Aquil·les el cos jove i despedaçat d'Hèctor.

EMPTY APARTMENT BUILDING IN SUMMER

The stairs are soundless
beside the elevator's noisy abyss.
Everyone's away.
The street seems half-empty.
The fridge's small tomato is a heartening
postcard of desire.
Look, we share at least
a fridge semi-stocked with lettuce,
and the thin thread of light
eclipsing our future.
Futile days lie ahead:
deceit's shadow, melancholy,
torment sweet or bitter like a line
drawn in the earth.
In your hair, there's a lingering
smell of paint,
while my hands are full
of useless farewells.
I relish the day's brilliance
and the body's,
with leftover fruit becoming
ever more fragrant as it dries—
so that in our wounding,
you won't haul me the callous way
Achilles' chariot once dragged
young Hector's broken body.

La mà de virgili

El combat és lent i sinuós,
un foc temporal dalt els pujols.
Les llances i dards de l'enemic
han delmat tan a poc a poc
els pares que ens protegien que,
gairebé sense adonar-nos-en,
ens trobem, silents, esbatanats,
en els fogars de primera línia.
Fins aquí la mà de Virgili.
D'ara endavant el món serà distint:
serem sols contra l'incendi.
Sense guies, enduts només
pel secret tempteig del bon sentit,
comprendrem potser que els murs
de la fortalesa, els enemics i la guerra,
sols són ombres agegantades
d'un foc que és claror i és cendra.
El purgatori i el paradís són en nosaltres.

Virgil's Hand

The battle's slow and sinuous,
a stormy fire on the hilltops.
The enemy's spears and darts
have decimated,
at such a snail's pace,
our once-protecting parents,
that, almost unawares, we're caught,
wordless, shield-less, in the blazing
tumult of the frontline.
Up till now, Virgil's hand.
From this day forward,
the world will be utterly different:
we'll combat the fire
totally on our own.
Guideless, spurred by a secret
quest for common sense,
perhaps, in the long run, we'll realize
the ramparts,
the enemy, the war itself,
are trumped-up shadows
of a fire that's merely
light and ash;
we'll realize: purgatory
and paradise reside
entirely within us.

Pluja

Quan ja ens avesàvem al bon temps
congries la tempesta, pluja sobtada,
i emmascares d'ombra la campana del cel
tallant-li a la tarda els seus colors.
Però tot diu que aquest aiguat inclement
que regalima i creix, i sembla un riu
arravatat i furient que tot ho nega,
potser durarà uns instants, només.
Així vols recordar-nos que tot mor,
que encara que la vida sigui benigna
com aquesta estantissa xafogor de plom
també les passions s'esvaeixen, furtives.
Que aquest xàfec lletós, fred, gris,
abans que el dia fosc s'ajaci
serà la gota suspesa del fullam convuls
on veurem, nítida sota la claror que mor,
la fragilitat del temps que ens arrossega.

Rain

Just when we'd gotten accustomed
to clement weather,
you whip up a cloudburst,
un-forecast drops,
and mask with shadows,
the vaulted sky, eliminating
the afternoon's colors.
Yet all things imply
this river-like, merciless shower,
swelling and overflowing,
ruthless, heedless, enraged,
will most likely endure
no more than a few minutes—
your way of reminding us
everything dies,
that life's benign
as this muggy stillness,
your way of insisting
even passions that appear
obdurate as iron
are fleeting, short-lived.
Before the dim day
heads back to its lair,
this chilly, gray, milky shower,
will dwindle down
to a raindrop clinging
to tumultuous, wind-whipped foliage,
so that we can grasp,
in the dying light,
with crystal clarity,
un-mighty time towing us along.

Taxidermista

Vés fins al fons del tapís de palmeres,
fins a aquest aparador obagós de somnis
on el temps ha despullat els seus costums
en un carnestoltes de bèsties dissecades.
—Quants de records t'assalten en veure
la canalla amb el nas aixafat al vidre!
Tira una moneda, ulls clucs, i veuràs
com les bèsties abandonen el badall d'avorriment
i comenten amb xiscles vermells, brutals,
entre ullals corcats i pells arnades,
que malament envellim els homes
bellugant com belluguem, frisosos de neguit,
calbs, quequejants, comatosos,
dins la nostra mesquina gàbia de vidre.

Taxidermist

Go to the end of the carpet
with its patterned palm trees,
as far as the display case,
shadowy with dreams,
where time has stripped away customs
in a raucous carnival of stuffed animals.
Countless memories surface when you witness
kids pressing their noses to the glass!
Toss a coin, eyes closed, and you'll see
the moth-eaten beasts depart,
apathetic, yawning, commenting,
with red maws and ruined teeth,
on how unpleasantly men age,
while fretfully, anxiously, we mill about,
hairless, stuttering, nodding as if comatose,
in our mean glass cage.

A LA MANERA D'ANNE SEXTON

El fons del pou és fosc i sense por
perquè és finit.
Com el fons del teu cos i del meu cos
és segur i és lluminós
perquè és finit.
Però la pell que no ens podem arrencar
és la d'altre:
un desert que són paraules.
La meva primera imatge
o els ulls que no arribo a copsar
em són la sang dels límits.
I la veu que em diu el nom
és la distància i és silenci.
I les ungles que esgarrapen
són el temps que separa
tots aquests dies que el llapis va marcant:
fa divuit dies que t'espero.

AFTER ANNE SEXTON

The well-bottom's shadowy and fearless,
because it's finite.
Like the depth of your body and mine,
also luminous and firm,
because it's finite.
But the skin we can't part with
is the other's skin,
a desert fashioned of words.
My first, fresh image of you,
or your ever-elusive eyes
are, for me,
the very essence of limits.
The voice uttering my name
becomes distance
and *is* silence.
And the plaintive fingernails
which scrape and scratch
are the time periods separating
all those pencil-marked dates:
it's been eighteen whole days
without you.

ARBRE VELL: II

El que hi havia en l'arbre, hi és;
perquè tot allò que fou, és.
Només cal la mà que hi descansa
i que li diu: "vine".
Perquè la mà és ell: arbre i pensament
i temps que et vol i et busca
per sobreviure en tu
perquè si penses el ser, ets;
i, si penses el buit del ser, ets el buit.
Causalitat.
Acosta la mà per donar-me certesa,
gairebé com si voler i ser
haguessin d'ajuntar-se als llavis
on som, nosaltres, arbre.
On jo sóc la teva escorça
i tu el buit que em crema.

OLD TREE: II

What thrived in the tree still lingers,
for everything that was
remains.
Rather like the resting hand
murmuring: *come.*
Because the hand's synonymous
with the man himself:
tree and thought
craving and seeking
to survive in you,
for if you contemplate being,
you exist,
and if you consider
the notion of life's emptiness
you're reduced to emptiness.
Causality.
The hand approaches
to reward me with certainty,
almost as if being and desire
accumulated on our lips,
where we are, in truth,
the tree.
Where I am your bark,
and you, a burning emptiness
lodged within me.

CALIPSO

Durant set anys—¿o foren cinc?—
la nimfa divina entre dees
li ha ofert menges, oblit,
una passió compartida.
Vora l'espluga on Calipso habita
hi creixen verns i xiprers,
una parra de vi ufanosa
—tot el que els mortals delita.
Un coneixement, emperò, manca a la nimfa:
ni que sigui en una illa balmada,
i amb una amant en delícies divina,
cap mortal no s'avindrà mai a aceptar
una fatigosíssima eternitat de joventut i bellesa,
mancada d'allò que els homes més aprecien:
el design inassolit, el record inassolible.

CALYPSO

For seven years—or was it five?—
the divine nymph plied him with
forgetfulness, delicacies, shared passion.
Near Calypso's grotto,
cypresses and alders grew, a grapevine
for fashioning luxuriant wine
—all that tantalizes men.
A truism lost on the nymph:
not even on an island
adorned with caves,
in the arms of a supernal lover
can a mere mortal endure
a wearying eternity
of youth and beauty,
devoid of what men prize most:
elusive memory,
unattainable desire.

SIBIL·LA

Hores petites. Sentim els passos en silenci.
Ara la sibil·la recita els seus errors—
presagis quequejants al fons d'un pou enterbolit.
Vés i regateja, poeta que desconfies del teu cor;
que et digui quin és el preu del somni.
Tant se'ns en donen les ombres del futur,
el que volem és engrapar-les, certes,
que no ens fugin, escàpoles, dels dits
com aquesta escletxa de llum sota la porta.
Dir «hivern» i veure la neu dels anys que ens abalteix,
llançar monedes a l'estany i ser estimats,
saber que, a cada mot que la sibil·la diu,
un esclau anhelant redimeix el jou antic
o un general guanya, per fi, el seu imperi.
Que el seu oracle ens dugui el dring de tot desig
i als silencis advertim, en un llambreig,
el broll on l'aigua mansa s'esclarissa
sota la bonior envescada dels til·lers.
No cal que hi hagi cap futur, tot és aquí—
el món cruel, l'amor que et vol somriure—,
encara que tu mateix no en vegis les certeses
i hagis d'esperar l'oracle obscur per adonar-te
que el mirall opac del cor te les entela.

SIBYL

Late night. Let's listen to her approach
in silence:
Now the sibyl proclaims
your failures—
stuttering portents in the depths
of a troubled well—
see them and contest them, poet,
mistrustful of your own heart;
let me tell you
the price of dreaming.
The future's phantoms,
what do they give us?
Our goal's to seize them firmly,
to prevent them from fleeing,
fugitive, out of our hands,
like this crack of light
slipping beneath the door.
We long to say "winter"
and witness how the snow of the years
stirs us to sleep;
we crave to lob coins in the pool
and be loved,
to be sure that, with every word
the sibyl intones,
a panting slave gains his freedom
at the ancient games
or a general attains, at long last,
his empire.
Let the oracle call forth
murmurs of desire
and, amid the silences, let's notice,
at a glance, the stream

of gentle water rinsing itself
beneath the sticky limes' rustling.

No future's required, everything's here—
the callous world, the love
that induces you to smile—
even though you can't discern
any certainties yourself
and must linger, waiting for
the cryptic oracle to report
everything your heart's cloudy mirror
obscures from you.

L'EMPERADOR ADRIÀ MEDITA SOBRE L'EDAT D'OR

d'après M. Yourcenar

Som teixidors que sargim les robes d'un vell ordre.
No hi ha res més i, en el costum, imitem
les arts i els llibres dels antics mestres.
Però ho sabem: avui no hi ha ningú
comparable a Praxíteles, Aristòtil o Arquimedes.
A l'àgora s'apleguen, bruts i espellifats,
els soldats que paguem perquè fingeixin lluitar
contra un enemic desconegut, que els és idèntic.
Allò que ens ensenyaren s'acaba i la memòria ens pesa.
Consolem-nos: aquests que han de detrossar-nos
atiats per falsos profetes, en referir-se a nosaltres
parlaran d'una edat d'or pretèrita.

THE EMPEROR HADRIAN MUSES ON THE GOLDEN AGE

after Marguerite Yourcenar

We're weavers mending robes
of an old order, nothing more,
and, in our customs, we mimic
the art and literature of old masters.
But it's clear to us: nowadays there's no match
for Praxiteles, Aristotle, or Archimedes.
The ragged and brutish crowd the agora,
mercenaries paid to feign
struggle with an unknown enemy,
indistinguishable from them.
True instruction has ceased
and memory is onerous.
Only this consoles us:
stirred by false prophets,
those to blame for our future ruin,
will surely refer to us, in time,
as figures of a bygone golden age.

CEMENTIRI A L'ERMITA DE SANTA EULÀLIA D'ALENDO

Fa cent anys dos infants jugaven
en aquest tros de terra. Hi dibuixaven
rectangles partits pel llarg
i hi clavaven la navalla del futur
amb la sorpresa maldestra de la infància.
—Em toca el cel.
—I a mi, l'infern.
Així tallaven en porcions més menudes
el fang amb què es va crear el món.
Ara que passegem pel cementiri
penso si algú haurà trobat mai
entre les mans lligades d'un cadàver
la navalla rovellada que dorm
en aquest equador on les arrels
fan girar el món.
Mentrestant apleguem els llumenets rojos
de la moixera de guilla,
i al palmell són boles de fang
que ressusciten en silenci.

Cemetery At The Chapel Of Saint Eulalia d'Alendo

A century ago two kids played
on this bit of land. They drew
rectangles, then divvied them up,
clasping the pen-knife of the future
with a boy's awkwardness and amazement.
—I'll take heaven
—And I'll take hell.
In this way the two proceeded to cut,
in ever-smaller portions,
mud used to fashion
the world's property.
Passing the cemetery,
I wager if someone's unearthed,
that between the corpse's tethered hands,
they'll find a rusty pen-knife resting
in this equator where the roots
make the world revolve.
While we cull red lamps
belonging to a mountain ash,
in our palms, they become clay marbles
from our boyish horseplay, suddenly
coming back to life in silence.

OBJECTES

Allò que més va costar de decidir
va ser que li traguessin l'anell;
no perquè tingués cap valor especial
o s'hagués de fondre al crematori,
sinó perquè la mare pogués tenir
algun record tangible. Hi penso ara
que veig l'arracada al costat del llit:
un altre objecte que m'és estrany
i que és una part de tu. Ens preocupa
que el petit no se la fiqui a la boca, però envejo
aquestes coses, més enllà dels sentiments;
fredes sempre i sempre pròximes i nostres.
Com un hoste adquirit i complaent
amb qui no discutim, instal·lat per sempre
allà on no cal misteri: al lòbul jove,
al turmell adolescent, als dits dels morts.
Que en aquestes ratlles que et deixo
hi trobis, doncs, els mots desats amb cura:
només meus, secrets, perquè els obris
quan el foc se t'endugui els meus records.

OBJECTS

The toughest decision:
determining the ring's fate,
not due to any special value
that would make it a shame
to consign it to
the crematorium's blast,
but because Mother might retain
some tangible memory.
I ponder it now that I spy
an earring lodged by the bed:
another object that seems
suddenly odd but part of you.
We're worried our little one
might slip it into his mouth,
but I'm envious of these
dispassionate objects;
forever chilly, intimate,
very much our own—
like an acquired, malleable guest
who goes unmentioned,
installed for good
there where mysteries aren't even needed:
on a youthful earlobe,
an adolescent ankle,
on a dead man's fingers.
In these left-behind lines, you'll find
words lovingly kept,
secrets belonging solely to me,
my legacy for you to read
when the flames have purged
all trace of me
from your memory.

El prat

Acabats de plantar, ha fet lligar un cartonet
al tronc de tots els arbres. I us els ensenya:
un arbre per a cada nét, i besnét, un prat
perquè un dia hi vinguin, una memòria vegetal
que us veurà créixer. Perquè s'alimentin
dels records sota les pedres o, si l'any ha estat bo,
allarguin la mà al cel o s'afanyin a recollir
el fruit prohibit que l'experiènca
encara no ha tingut temps de fer malbé.
Però potser, més senzill, allò que vol
és sortir ella, la que us ha plantat els arbres,
de les cendres profundes i, arrels amunt,
asseure's a la vostra boca—poma dolça,
nou verda i aspra—i contemplar el prat alt
i el flux lent del les marees que oscil·len,
bellíssimes, com l'alè lent de somni,
per fer-nos comprendre que el llot marronós
de decepcions i culpes és també el perdó
feliç i antic que ens hi ha plantat per sempre.

THE ORCHARD

After the planting's done,
she fastens a cardboard label
to every tree trunk, then proffers
one for each grandchild
and great grandchild, an orchard
for them to savor someday, a tribute
in foliage that will stand guard
over the family's growth.
In this way, her heirs will feed
on stone-cached memories,
or, if it's been favorable, a trophy year,
they'll lift their hands heavenward
or fret about the surest way
to pick and treasure the forbidden fruit
experience has yet to turn sour.
Though I suspect
that this diligent planter's true desire
(and this would be simpler)
is to bloom herself,
to rise from subterranean ash
up through roots,
to nestle in the rugged walnut,
the dulcet green apple's mouth—
to admire the elevated orchard
and the tides' languid arrival,
as she waves, so deftly, gorgeously,
like sleep's slow-paced breathing,
to make us grasp:
the mire, the ooze
of guilt and deceit's also
the steady, joyous forgiveness
she's planted and left to us
forever.

POSTA

El capaltard és un calidoscopi
que giravolta amb dits sanguinolents
en la bellesa fràgil del vitrall.
Gira el vent, rogallós, i és oreig
que agonitza, rogenc i esgroguissat.
Tota realitat muda i es fon
com el sol que contemplo esbalaït:
aquest sol fugisser, morat, blavís,
que es vincla i s'esfilagarsa, aspriu,
entre l'olor lenta del maig i la teia
que el grava, perdurable, a la memòria.
¡Quanta, quanta riquesa en cada instant!
Ara mateix, l'atzar de la retina
serà per sempre aquest infant que salta
l'aigua tèpida d'uns tolls enfangats,
bru i colrat, banyat d'un or vermell,
com figura morta, tot color,
petrificada en mots iridiscents
al marbre blanc i negre del poema.

SUNSET

Sunset's a kaleidoscope
worked by blood-daubed fingers,
something glimpsed through delicate,
lovely stained glass.
All raspy vocals, the wind shifts—
a doomed breeze,
russet alloyed with yellow.
Reality seems to melt and mutate,
as does the sun
I witness in awe:
a violet, bruised, vanishing sun,
that stretches and frays,
like something wild,
between May's abiding scent
and the torch that inscribes it
indelibly on my memory.
Each moment, full as a cornucopia!
Even now the random
image on my retina
will remain forever
this small boy jumping
muddy, tepid puddles,
his skin bronzed and dark, bathed
in a riot of red-gold:
a still life, suffused with color,
fixed in iridescent words
on the black and white
marble of the poem.

PASTÍS DE FANG

L'aigua que raja sense esglai d'aquesta mànega vella
forma un safareig transparent d'esperança clara.
Els tolls del jardí ens la xuclen amb la mateixa set de saber
que té la veritat interminable, i els infants despullats
vénen a regirar l'impossible amb branquillons insomnes,
dits de farina i galledes del color d'ocells exòtics.
Cada pastís és pastat en un petit palmell de fang,
i el cel blavíssim i els brins d'herba també són
"el món en son primer matí," sortint del caos
—una existència sense buits i sense errors, no enterbolida.
Mai més l'obra omnipotent dels déus no tornarà a tenir
aquesta senzilla meravella, clara i transcendent,
que construeix un mercat de fang i d'arbres foscos.
Comparant pastissos comparen el seu poder naixent,
la realitat d'allò que seran i que repetiran per sempre:
la por a la fosca, l'onada eterna, l'amor incomprensible.
I nosaltres, déus poderosos, que els espiem mig amagats
darrere l'ombra fidel d'afirmacions que ens oculten la derrota,
també veiem cada costella que naixerà del fang.
Quan els infants s'adormin cansats d'imitar el món,
el caprici atrabiliari de l'atzar ens deixarà només
engrunes de sorra seca, les paraules petites d'aquest joc:
un matí de vida nua que brilla, convulsa,
com un bocí d'ampolla brilla enmig de l'herba negra.

MUD PIE

The gush pouring fearlessly from this old hose
forms a see-through basin of bright water.
Naked children are playing
around slow-sipping garden pools,
with a similar thirst for knowledge,
a thirst that makes the quest for truth unending;
once again, they've come to stir up
impossibility, with never-sleeping twigs,
flour-dipped fingers, and pails
the colors of exotic birds.
Each pie is kneaded with a tiny
palm-sized share of mud,
and the bluest of skies
and minute blades of grass
are also "the world on the very first morning,"
an exit from chaos—an existence
lacking emptiness or errors,
bereft of muddiness.
Nevermore will the gods' almighty work
turn out to possess
such marvelous simplicity,
lucent and transcendent,
as the children construct a marketplace
out of mud and dark trees.
Comparing little pies,
they compare their own burgeoning power
with the reality that the terror
of darkness and undying waves,
of unfathomable love,
will forever exist
and go on repeating.
And we, the puissant gods,

who spy on the children,
partly envious,
from the obstinate shadow of the affirmations
that obscure defeat,
see, as well, each rib
destined to be born from the mud.
When the kids doze at last,
weary of imitating the world,
capricious, ill-tempered fate's
legacy will be merely
grains of dry sand,
only the little words of their game:
the memento of a glistening morning,
naked and alive,
bright as a bottle shard,
a beacon amid darkened grass.

EL MEU FILL ASSEGUT EN UN RACÓ D'UN RESTAURANT D'AQUÍ A CINQUANTA ANYS

D'aquí a cinquanta anys, aquest home
que seu a la taula del costat, a Viena,
seràs tu que ara seus entre bolquers.
Mira-te'l com és felic i ric amb poc,
regirant els seus records en aquest racó soliu
ben al fons del restaurant, mentre tira molles de pa
dins el plat de sopa caldosa que fumeja.
Se'l veu que frueix, com jo, d'un únic moment sol
i se'n delita, i abraça aquesta llum verdosenca
i sense culpa de la tarda que taca la ciutat
com qui afina la corda vella i tesa d'un violí.
D'aquí a cinquanta anys, abstret en un racó llunyà,
recordaràs, com ell, un carrusel de llum blavosa
dins una migdiada d'infant, o el cos de mel
d'una dona que et va estimar dins una barca,
i la memòria entelada t'endreçarà, a poc a poc, les coses.
Sabràs que cal destriar el dolor de la por,
i la passió del joc que ara mateix enfila amunt
aquesta roda que omple el cel del Prater.
¿No sents ja la música alegre del carrilló
que tapa a penes el xiulet de l'enemic?
Doncs pensa que aquest home escriu també
per fer-me escriure a mi, i que jo escric
perquè aquest instant petitament feliç sigui
una mà amable que s'encalla al teu record de mi.

Imagining My Son, Seated In The Corner Of This Eatery In Fifty Years

Fifty years from now, this man
I spot at a Viennese table,
is who I dream you'll be,
dear you, currently in diapers.
See how elated he is,
and a tad rich,
sifting through memories
in this eatery's isolated corner,
while dipping bread
into a steamy soup bowl.
As afternoon stains the city,
notice he flourishes, as I do,
from a rare solitary moment,
guiltlessly embracing and relishing
this green-tinted light—
like a musician re-tuning
an old violin's taut strings.
Fifty years from now, right here
in an out-of-the-way corner,
tucked away like him, you'll recall
a blue-lit carousel
hidden within a baby's nap,
or the honey-sweet body
of a woman who loved you
on a boat-ride,
and, little by little,
the not totally tarnished memory
will put things in order for you.
You'll learn to detect
the pain lurking behind fear,
determine the passionate

within the playful.
A Ferris wheel fills the sky now,
above Prater's midway.
Don't you hear the lively music
of the wind-chimes that barely muffles
the enemy's whistle?
Let's suppose the corner man scribbles
to spur my work, too,
and that I write because,
at this small, upbeat moment, you follow
my safeguarding hand
to usher you past
your iconic and stranded memory of me.

CAPSA DE MISTOS

Quan és tèrbol el pes d'aquells que et vénen,
salva aquest record com qui salva per atzar
del turment inútil un objecte de les golfes:
una capseta de mistos, feta de fusta i de paper.

Això, que va ser presó temible dels insects
i cofre violat d'algun tresor secret,
t'obre els barrots goluts de la memòria
a les monedes emboirades del present.

Potser si fregaves amb dits fosforescents
s'encendria de nou aquella humida olor
de les nits plenes de l'estiu,
i veuries ballar—com titelles siamesos—
aquells mistos consumits per l'escalf d'una passió
més efímera en la flama que en la cendra.

Que no eren cap truc ho saps ara en solitari,
en atorgar-los una existència que és ben teva
amb signes que són la condició dels homes.
No et pot enganyar la capseta de fusta i de paper
plena de caps que aquell foc va contorçar.

Són llances cremades, mans envellides en la guerra,
que un dia—quan l'últim llumí cremi fins al dit
i ungla endins s'arrapi el cap amb ira humana—
et recordaran que amb aquests mistos encens també
la flama blava del petit fogó on ara escalfes
la llet de l'infant que marxa a escola.

MATCHBOX

Keep this souvenir,
when your sense of the past blurs,
just as you might salvage something
cluttering the attic.
Don't toss out this matchbox
of wood and paper.

Once an insect's dreaded prison,
a coffin desecrated
for some secret treasure,
now the match box pries open
memory's greedy bars, proffering
the present's misted coins.

If you strike the box
with phosphorescent fingers,
maybe you'll re-ignite
the smell of sweltering summer nights
when you set the matches dancing—
like miniature Siamese twins:
consumed by a fiery passion
more fleeting as flame
than as ash.

The matches were never
a mere magic trick, you realize,
and grant them an existence
similar to yours,
linked to the human condition.
It can't possibly trip you up—
the little wood and paper box

full of matches the fire crumpled.
They're war-withered hands,
burnt swords
able to remind you someday
—as the last brief light burns
down to your fingernail,
snatching the tip
with a human fury—
that they also spark the burner's
blue flame meant to warm up
the milk of the little boy
marching intently off to school.

Gossos

Mireu-los: són una colla de gossos rònecs
acostumats a envair, a fonyar jardins.
Freds, desvergonyits, res no els detura
—ni aquest grup de poetes que malda, també,
per donat sentit a la vergonya de la vida.
Coixos, orbs, nafrats de paparres,
encara ensumen amb llur fúria esmorteïda
la gossa vell que habita aquest jardí.
I això que ens importuna, ens els acosta:
animals impúdics, fidels, envilits,
que, com nosaltres, assetgen, furients o defallits,
la quimera de l'amor: un poder suprem
que, anorreant-los, els pugui redimir.

Dogs

Keen trespassers trampling flowerbeds,
they're a pack of mangy dogs;
look at them: cold, immoderate,
nothing curbs their roaming—
not even this band of poets
also striving
to make meaning of life's shame.
Blind, tumbledown, tick-bedeviled,
yet they still sniff,
with muffled fury,
at the old she-dog,
tenant of this yard.
But what begs to us
binds us to them:
shameless, loyal, reviled,
beasts, like us, that mount
furious or half-hearted assault
against love's insanity:
supreme power
upending and redeeming them
in the same breath.

Retaule à the cloisters

Per a vosaltres el món era un passatge forçat,
camí de salvació o d'infinita condemna
—com el gos d'aquest retaule que ha de córrer
travessant tot el mercat, un tall de carn a la boca.
Nosaltres, però, no esperem res. No tenim
dimonis ni sers alats que vetllin vora el coixí
per disputar-nos les ànimes en una llarga contesa.
El nostre apocalipsi és allò que ens és donat:
gratacels, llums, insomnis, ponts de ferro.
Com us envegem la pau d'aquesta pintura bella
on l'espiga i la rosella s'enamoren. El vostre temps
s'ha detingut en aquesta cicatriu de la memòria.
Viviu com viu el que és etern i el que és inútil.
I jo us envejo la vida i em pregunto si algun dia
seré també com el drac, l'unicorn o el porc senglar:
un fantasma del temps que guaita des d'un retaule
els rostres des visitants que la mort li envia.

Altarpiece At "The Cloisters"

The world, for you,
was a forced pilgrimage, a trek
to absolution or endless punishment—
like this altarpiece dog
scurrying the market's length,
a slab of meat in his mouth.
We, on the other hand,
don't hope for anything.
We have no devils,
no winged and hovering beings
near our pillows,
watchful, eager to wage
a longstanding battle for our souls.
Our here-and-now apocalypse
has been meted out:
skyscrapers, bright lights,
insomnia, steel bridges.
How we crave
this marvelous painting's serenity,
where a poppy's enamored
with an ear of wheat.
Your era's stilled, conserved
in this scar of memory.
You live as the useless
and eternal live.
And I envy your life and wonder
if someday I'll also be brother to
the dragon, the unicorn,
or the wild boar:
a ghost of time peering
from an altarpiece
at the faces of visitors
death sends his way.

MÀ TALLADA

Talla'm la mà
que és tota teva,
i fes que la pell, la carn, les ungles
siguin aquest record antic:
una nena que esmorza,
sola, davant la tele.
Ara que la nit esquerpa
m'és un vidre tot de pors
i de desfici, tanca'm les parpelles
perquè no vegi tanta solitud i,
molt a poc a poc, avisa'm
quan vingui l'alba i recompongui els vidres
i les mans amb què ens lliguem,
desesperadament, a la llum
tèbia i amorosida de cada mot.

Severed Hand

Cut off my hand,
it's all yours,
and transform my fingertips and flesh
into this old but unfading memory:
a solitary girl at her breakfast,
perched in front of the TV.
Now that the hostile night
is a glass, fashioned of fear
and unease, close my lids,
so I can't witness
this extravagant loneliness,
and slowly, slowly, let me know
when dawn blooms and composes again
the window panes and the hands
we once utilized
to bind each other
so desperately,
in the tepid, softened light
of every word.

El menja-pecats

Aquesta llum que imagines com aigua negra
d'un oceà tempestuós és la llum de la pietat humana.
En aquest vaixell adormit i vell d'una novel·la,
amb mariners, oficials i velam esquinçat pel vent feréstec,
l'infeliç de llavi leporí que agonitza sota coberta
commou com el silenci nou en una casa
que, al fons dels ulls, ens sembla acabada de parar.
Obre, trist, aquesta finestra que vols més lliure:
"Quan en un poble algú moria, l'anaven a buscar
i posaven un tros de pa al pit de l'home mort,
que el menja-pecats mastegava tot carregant, així,
amb els pecats comesos pel difunt." Mastega, doncs,
    el llenguatge
com qui obre la mirada perduda a un costum color de sang.
Una mateixa sang, la de les noies amb les cuixes tacades
i la d'un parrac humà que un passant duu en braços
—una mateixa sang, regalimant, color de llengua morta—.
Aquestes molles de pa que els morts t'ofereixen sense pressa
són les ombres que projecten la teva paga falsa.
Corre, com el menja-pecats, estrenyent a la mà
els vidres que es dessagnen, i tu mateix, color de por,
intenta fugir sota la pluja. Sempre hi ha una nit
per fer algú fora de casa, per escopir a un fugitiu,
per tirar pedres al pobre desgraciat que se'ns escapa
havent menjat els pecats d'un altre. Tots som culpables,
mentre el captaire ximple es perd en la nit—lliure
    i innocent—
fins que el tornin a cridar a una altra casa.
Anyell de déu que rentes els pecats del món . . .

THE SIN-EATER

based on a passage in Patrick O'Brian's Master and Commander

It's the radiance of human piety—
this light you envision
as a tempest-tossed sea's
black water.
On this old, drowsy night-time ship,
out of a tale of seamen, officers, and sails
rent by raging wind,
there's a grim, leprous lip
in egregious misery
under the covers,
harrowing as new silence
in a house, that seems,
from our vantage,
on the verge of collapse.
Please open, in wistful fashion,
this window begging for release:
"When a villager died,
they'd place on the corpse's heart
a bit of bread
for the sin-eater to devour
the dead's countless sins."
Devour then, this language
opening a long-lost gaze
at a blood-hued uniform.
The blood belonging
to girls with stained thighs
is a synonym for what
the runaway human rag
carried in his arms—
blood the color

of a motionless tongue.
These bits of bread
the dead proffer impassively
are the shadows that project
your counterfeit payment.
Run, like the sin-eater,
deadset on fleeing in the rain,
gripping in your hand
blood-tainted glasses,
while you yourself grow
flooded with fear.
There's always a night
for booting someone out of the house,
for spitting on a fugitive,
for lobbing rocks
at the scurrying outcast
who has gorged on another's sins.
We're all guilty,
while the low-on-the-totem
beggar wanders,
a fly-by-night refugee—
blameless, free at last,
till he's back to wail
in still another house of mourning:
lamb of God washing away
the world's sins . . .

Setmana santa

Surt una mica ajupit del cotxe
i es redreça amb un gest, amb por
d'arrossegar els peus. Al forn
compra una barra de pa
que paga amb monedes d'un grapat
que duu a la butxaca.
Encén els llums de casa,
foragita l'ombra que ha deixat
tort el marc d'un quadre.
Canvia l'abric per un jersei vell.
Sopa davant la tele mentre fulleja
amb desesma un diari gratuït.
Despenja el telèfon per si hi té missatges;
obre i tanca la nevera buida.
La vida és una puta venjativa
que li passa comptes amb el verdet
brut d'una ràbia encalmada.
Existir és fosc, ja no xucla llet
d'una dona. Déu no existeix.
Ha mort el Fill; ara el Pare és sol.
Mals temps per a la lírica. Agafa
un ganivet i amb la tinta dels ulls
escriu aquest poema.

HOLY WEEK

Bending a little, he exits the car,
then straightens himself, mindful
not to shuffle. At the baker's
he purchases a loaf of bread,
with coins fished from a stash
at the bottom of his pocket.
He switches the lights on in his flat,
banishing a shadow that caused
a painting's frame to seem awry.
Sheds his coat and slips into an old jersey.
Has dinner opposite the TV, while gazing
listlessly at a free paper.
Grabs the phone to check for messages,
opens and closes the empty fridge.
Life is a vengeful whore
insisting he pay with the filthy
muck of stifled anger.
Existence means darkness;
he can't suckle
milk from a woman's breast anymore.
God is unreachable.
The Son is dead, and the Father, alone now.
Hard times for poetry. He takes a knife
and with the ink from his eyes
writes this poem.

ALESHORES

Aleshores amb les mans
li acaronava el cap,
aleshores amb els braços
li estrenyia el cos,
aleshores amb el dit
li arrencava els ulls,
aleshores amb les dents
li rosegava el fetge,
aleshores amb les urpes
li esqueixava els records,
aleshores amb els mugrons
l'amamantava amb llet d'odi,
aleshores amb la llengua
li deia Senyor, Senyor,
només ho faig per amor,
perquè ens has promès
que aquest pa és el teu cos
i aquest vi la teva sang.

Then

Then with her hands
she'd crown her son's head,
then with her arms
she'd embrace him,
then with her fingers
she'd pluck out his eyes,
then with her teeth
she'd gnaw his liver,
then with motherly claws
she'd shred his memories,
then with her nipples
she'd nourish him
on the milk of hatred,
then with her tongue,
she'd insist, Lord, Lord,
I'm only doing this for love,
because you've pledged
that this bread is your body
and this wine, your blood.

El lladre bo

Els claus, a dalt la creu, són un dolor insuportable.
El pes del cos m'esquinça el cos,
com un parrac xop de vinagre.
Ara els vull mal, però sobretot vull morir prest.
I a aquest que em parla, un boig que frega els vidres
dels cotxes que s'aturen davant un semàfor en vermell,
més val dir-li que sí. Creu que li parla el pare
i el pobre desvarieja. Però allò que m'acompanya
és que em recorda, enmig de tant dolor, el meu:
i com m'acomboiava entre els seus braços,
i com el feia riure amb els meus jocs,
i com, de nit, tossia a la màrfega del terra.
I sé que ell em perdona, i que comprèn la meva ira
per no voler morir i desitjar la mort abans que la tortura.
—No tornaré a trencar res més. Perdona'm, pare.
Allunya'm d'aquest pobre rei i el seu seguici,
i torna'm a carregar a coll, mig adormit,
fins a la màrfega apedaçada de la nostra casa molt humil.

The Good Thief

Unbearable: the cross's nails.
My body's heaviness
rends me, a rag
steeped in vinegar.
Now I'm eager to heap
indignities on my tormentors
but mostly I'm in a rush
to die soon.
And in answer to this messiah,
muttering like a madman
who washes windows of cars
idling at a red light,
well, you'd better say yes.
He thinks he's got
a direct line to God the Father,
but he's raving.
Amid his lunacy, what lingers
is a souvenir of my own dad,
my own troubles,
how he lifted me in his arms,
and chuckled at my games,
on his hard-luck mattress
laid on the floor.
And I know my Father forgives me
and understands my anger,
but I don't want to die;
it's better to give up the ghost
than be crucified.
—I'll never break anything else.
Forgive me, pops.
Save me from this pauper king
and his bunch,
hoist me on your back once more,
as you lounge, half conked out,
on our mean little shack's
patched-up mattress.

CELLER

Aquests homes que compacten el terra al capdavall del poble
per construir-hi un celler, i pis, i casa,
no són espectres que esperin reconeixement,
sinó anatomies animades en la distància remota.
Aixequen un safareig per trepitjar-hi el raïm,
vora l'eixida, i encimenten el pas a la comuna.
Hi neix gent, dinen, passen els anys, moren.
Són uns altres temps, colonitzats, tristos, pròspers:
hi ha electricitat i una centraleta de telèfons,
canten els grills a l'estiu.
Si en un bateig no hi ha confits
la canalla cridem que el nen es morirà.
Els dies són giragonses de sang,
plou i tots resen a Santa Bàrbara bendita.
La vinya és petita, menestral, blava,
la tarda una llesca de pa amb vi sucre.
La tia àvia que toca la campaneta pels reis
s'apaga a casa, fosa, com un migdia d'oli.
La família creix, mor, s'escampa, oblida:
el món es un sínia rodona. El terra del celler fangueja,
les bótes formen construccions fortificades,
la memòria són reguerols de vi.

Tot això existeix perquè, molts anys després,
el meu germà i jo ensumem un guant
que ha estat dut en una altra verema
i recordem la mateixa olor agra de most
al celler de Gelida. L'olor esdevé pupil·la del temps
i dóna a tots aquests personatges la perfecció
d'una alcova que algú acaba d'emblanquinar.
Amb calç a les mans, som un mirall
al fons del riu on altres miren sense veure'ns.

CELLAR

These earth-tamping men
aren't attention-seeking ghosts,
fashioning a cellar, a flat, a house,
near the front of town,
but spirited bodies,
in the remote distance.
They erect a tub
for grape trampling,
and behind the house, by the patio,
cement steps leading to a latrine.
People are born, they have dinner,
years go by, they die;
these are different times,
colonized, prosperous, melancholy:
electricity has arrived, summer crickets,
and a telephone switchboard.
At a baptism,
if grown-ups don't scatter
giveaway candies,
the local kids claim,
the baptized kid's "done for."
The days meander,
coursing with blood,
and everyone prays
to blessed Saint Barbara.
The vineyard's a small affair,
workmanlike, blue,
the afternoon a bread slice
wolfed down with wine and sugar.
My great aunt who always rang,
at Epiphany,

the little bell for the Three Kings,
fades away at home, melting
like an oily midday,
while the family expands,
dies, spreads, and forgets:
the world's a revolving waterwheel.
The cellar earth grows muddy,
turning casks to fortresses;
memory forms rivulets of wine.

All these events exist
because, many years afterward,
my brother and I sniffed
a glove grown hard
in a previous grape harvest,
and it conjured the identical smell
of unfermented grape juice
in the old cellar at Gelida.
The odor becomes like
time's vast pupil,
making the long-ago
keen again,
imbuing all those villagers
with the perfection of an alcove
just whitewashed.
With lime-gloved hands,
we're a mirror embedded
in the river bottom,
where strangers peer,
never seeing us.

VIENA, NADAL 1939

La dona més gran és gairebé cega
i acaba de complir noranta anys;
la filla petita, que li estreny el braç,
ja passa dels seixanta. Sou a Viena,
i per aquestes escales decorades pel Nadal
heu de baixar amb neguit i sentir en silence
l'eco de les botes de la Wehrmacht.
Dues dones soles, doncs,
que, atemorides, deixen enrere tapets i bibelots,
lectures en veu alta, partitures i fotos,
que ocupen d'ençà d'anys un lloc tan inalterable
com les ordres escrites i els segells encara humits
amb què els botxins i els obedients es justifiquen.
Tant se val si al camp és temps de fer fogueres
o si al carrer festiu hi ha gent i plou o neva.
Tant se val si elles compadeixen aquests joves
o si penseu que el noiet educat, en uniforme,
també voldria més manyaga la nit
que saben que se'ls acosta. Allò que ara veieu
és el braç de Caïm i el foc mesell a la platea
alçat contra l'espasa flamígera de l'àngel,
mentre voldríeu, com el rabadà infantil del teatrí
on bondat i fantasia s'agermanen d'innocència,
que també la història acabés bé i que triomfés
—abans d'abaixar-se la guillotina cruel d'aquest teló—
la justícia dels jueus, dels nens, del simples.

VIENNA, CHRISTMAS 1939

Just turned ninety,
the oldest woman's already blind;
her youngest daughter,
guiding her by the arm,
she's barely in her sixties.
Imagine you're in Vienna,
and must descend these stairs
adorned for Christmas,
anxious, hearing in the silence
the *Wehrmacht's* echoing boots.
Two solitary women,
petrified, leaving in their wake,
table runners and bibelots,
books read aloud, births, and photos,
which kept them engaged for decades,
in a place as inalterable
as the written orders and the stamp,
still damp to the touch,
symbols of the executioners'
and their followers' rationales.
It dosen't matter,
if, in the countryside,
they have to build a fire,
or if, in the holiday street,
there are crowds, rain, or snow.
It doesn't matter if they identify
with the young, or if they think
the well-brought-up boy in uniform,
wishes the night could be
more compassionate somehow
when he comes to arrest them.

Now they imagine all this
as the arm of Cain and the leprous
fire on the plain, raised
to subdue the angel's flaming sword,
and like a puerile shepherd boy
featured in a Christmas pantomime
in which fantasy
is cousin to innocence,
they're sure that history, in turn,
will end well—before a plunging guillotine
savages the play—
and that justice for children and Jews,
justice for the humble,
is sure to triumph.

ALEMANYA, FI DE LA SEGONA GUERRA

Aquest home gran que davant el públic narra
els últims dies de la guerra a Alemanya
és, de sobte, la mà del jugador
que desvela la pobresa de les cartes.
Era un nen i ni tan sols sabia què era perdre.
Ara n'evoca la vida mutilada i vol lligar la por
i l'esperança als sons de paraules que el van salvar:
un comodí irònic i cruel, un bufó de la sort.
Han passat molts anys i sap que potser és injust
amb ell mateix. Però tampoc renega de la por
que el va fer somiar. Lliga amb dits maldestres
els mocadors del record com aquella tropa
espellifada que repetia mots desconeguts
al fons d'un refugi a les fosques. Per fer màgica la veu.
Cantant. Sota el terror de les passades dels avions
que avancen aliats com espectres cap al cercle de la mort.
La corrua de criatures, vells i dones rellisca sobre el fang.
I no paren de cantar. Sols es fixen en el negre calcigat
de les herbes de la riba i canten allò que algú ha dit
que els pot salvar. No confien en la innocència,
confien en les paraules. Al capdavant de tot va el germà gran
que enlaira un pal amb els parracs de la bandera blanca.
I la lletania desesperada que xifra l'univers
en el so buit de cinc paraules: cendra de cendres,
cendres de dones i d'infants, cants i cendres.
we are women and children, uiarrbumananxildran,
ui-arr-buman-an-xildran, we are women and children . . .
Una compassió blava i impossible on es diposita el futur,
un càntic que demana sentit a la llengua dels altres.
Creiem en el barquer ferit o en el perdó que no calia.

GERMANY, THE END OF WORLD WAR II

This old man, recalling in public
the last gasp of Hitler's war,
is suddenly the player's hand revealing
the lowest cards in the deck.
Just a boy, he had no clue
what losing was like.
Now he evokes a havoc-ridden life,
and lives to braid fear and hope
with the rescuing sounds
of a foreign tongue:
as if he'd been dealt
some ill-fated jester,
a cruel, ironic joker.
Many years have passed
and he's learned
maybe he's been unjust,
too hard on himself.
Yet he doesn't disown the cowering
that spurred his dreaming.
With clumsy fingers he bundles
handkerchiefs of memory
—like the frayed crowd
he huddled among,
repeating unfamiliar words
in the depths of a refuge
plunged into darkness. Singing
to make magic happen.
Under the terror of the passing planes
advancing the Allies like phantoms
toward death's circle.
A welter of kids, old folks, and women

faltering in the mud.
Unable to stop singing,
focused only on the black trampling
of riverbank herbs,
singing because
someone promised them salvation,
not trusting in innocence
but in words.
At the head of them all,
his eldest brother raising
a pole with a tattered truce flag,
launching again their desperate,
sky-hurled litany,
encoded in five hollow words:
ashes to ashes,
ashes of women and children,
songs and ashes:
we are women and children,
wearewomenandchildren,
we-are-women-and-children,
we are women and children . . .
A chant begging meaning
to a strange tongue,
a chant begging for a blue,
impossible compassion
where the future eddies.
We put our faith
in the injured ferryman,
in never-needed mercy.

Nit clara

Fa una nit molt clara, immensa;
contemplo els estels, enllà dels pins,
i la negror insondable de la volta.
A baix, a la badia, tot són lluminàries
i la música dels bars encén el raucar de les granotes.
¿Quina mar hi ha darrere aquest teló
o són onades de paper que no acaben d'enganyar-nos?
S'empaiten, absurds, Capricorn i Sagitari,
l'Óssa Major enfonsa la celístia dins la mar,
canten les cigales i jo, sota el Dofí,
em sento ull únic que sotja i que comprèn
o insignificant engruna d'un àpat de pesombre.
Tornen les músiques, l'aroma dels garrofers,
el petarreig de les barques que surten a l'encesa;
enllà, parpellegen els estels com raïms d'or.
Allargo el braç, com si pogués abastar-los,
i per un moment, ebri, "m'inundo d'immens".

CLEAR NIGHT

On an immense, clear night, I ponder
stars looming above a stretch of pines,
the vaulted sky's endless blackness.
Below me, the bay's brimming
with bright lights, and music blaring
from the bars has ignited
a chorus of croaking frogs.
Behind this curtain, tell me,
is there really a sea?—
or just paper waves bereft
of any power to deceive us?
Capricorn and Sagittarius continue
their foolhardy pursuit,
and the Great Bear
submerges starlight into the sea.
And rooted beneath the Dolphin,
amid the cicadas' singing,
I imagine I'm the only watchful eye,
imbuing it all with meaning,
then wonder if I'm merely
an insignificant morsel
at a banquet table of crestfallen dreams.
Then they swim back to me:
drifting music, the carob's scent,
the crackle of small, lit-up boats
heading out to fish.
Beyond it all, flickering stars
like clusters of gold.
I reach out as if to pluck them,
and just for a moment,
I'm drunk with stars,
"drowning in immensity."

CEMENTIRI NEVAT

Cauen borrallons espessos. Tot calla.
Calla la nena que ha remogut el fossar
i la terra que no sap que ho és del cementiri.
Callen les espelmes amb animetes que flaquegen
i que has hagut de protegir amb paper d'alumini.
El vent glaçat és pertot, als dits vermells,
a les pregàries de les dones, a les pales
metàl·liques dels enterradors que es tapen
el cap amb bufandes velles. Aquí
la memòria és un escalf lletós, tímid,
com aquest cadàver que no recordes
si mai vas arribar a estimar.
La neu és blanca i és dins teu, per tot arreu.
Com un amor que encara no és mort
perquè ha quedat enganxat sota les arestes
de la pedra bruta, enfangada, de la vida.

SNOWY CEMETERY

Thick snowflakes fall,
hushing everything,
hushing the girl who's been
digging at the cemetery,
hushing the ground, which she didn't realize
was the earth of a graveyard,
hushing the candles' tiny,
flickering animas,
shielded with aluminum foil.
The icy wind's inescapable as it reaches
chafed fingers, matrons' prayers,
and glinting shovels
of gravediggers in hoary scarves
tamping the end.
Here memory evokes
a timid, cloudy warmth,
like the heat of a corpse you're not sure
you ever succeeded in loving.
The snow's everywhere at once,
even within you: a deep down white.
Like a love that refuses to die,
because it remains
glued, staunch under the rim
of the brute, mud-cloaked
rock of life.

RETRAT DEL POETA

Xiula el vent, l'aigua s'ha glaçat
a les canonades, neva.
Fa hores que és fosc
i es formen caramells de gel
a les teulades.
Que n'és de bo tancar el llibre,
bufar la bugia que crema sobre la taula
i, a la claror de la llar de foc,
arraulir-se al llit, sense sorolls,
per no desvetllar el son d'aquest cos jove
que ja fa estona que descansa, pur.
Ara, colgat sota les flassades, tanca
els ulls i rememora aquest dia
no gaire diferent de tots els altres.
Frueix d'aquest petit moment de plaer
que tot s'ho val, abandonant la mà
sobre un pit que sospira, adormit,
la cara en la tofa flonja dels cabells.
¿Serà així, la mort?
¿Benvinguda com aquesta son que et pren,
dolcíssima, sense retrets ni greuges,
agraint només els dons incommensurables de la vida?
¿Serà així que, en el camí de la fosca,
anirem a l'encontre de la llum?

Portrait Of The Poet

Freezing pipes, icicles
tapering from the eaves
in the blizzard's howling wind.
After a long bout of darkness,
it's a minor blessing
to close your book,
to snuff out the table candle,
and, under the glow of the fireplace,
to nestle in bed,
soundlessly, never stirring
the young body by your side,
dozing in all its purity.
Blanket-buried, close your lids,
re-enact this not uncommon day.
Relish this tiny, elating moment
that ennobles everything,
as you cup her sighing breast,
your face lost, entangled among
her hair's fluent, soft strands.
Will death be this way?
Welcome, like this drowsiness
you succumb to,
this sensation of sheer mildness,
without reproach or lament,
this uncluttered gratitude
for life's hard-to-measure gifts?
Will it be like this—
that on our way to darkness,
we'll encounter light?

Postscript 2018: Francesc Parcerisas And Embattled Catalonia

To meet Francesc Parcerisas, Catalonia's premier poet, and to learn more about last fall's disastrous referendum for independence that led to police violence and the political exile and imprisonment of key Catalan leaders, I return to Barcelona after half a decade. Given the shock and gravity of recent events in Catalonia and the fact that the bulk of the work on *Still Life with Children* was done in 2006 and 2007, I felt a postscript and update to this volume was essential.

Parcerisas, the august but always affable poet ("he reminds me of a Russian prince," a mutual friend says) graciously whisks me away from the El Prat airport to his summer apartment in Vilanova i La Geltrú, not far from the much more famous watering spot of Sitges. It's June 23, La Revetlla or La Nit de San Joan (The Night or Eve of Saint John the Baptist), and there are traditional holiday cakes and delicious pastries in the resort town's queue-filled bakeries, and after dusk, raucous firecrackers, showy fireworks, and customary beachfront bonfires ("Saint John's fires," meant to repel witches and evil spirits) to celebrate the baptizing saint's feast day and summer's exhilarating start. I've returned to a "small homeland" of bright acacias and eye-catching yellow ribbons everywhere (a sobering emblem of solidarity with Catalan political prisoners), and of course, the marigold and crimson of the Catalan flag draped over wrought-iron balconies and Mediterranean terraces. "Welcome to occupied Catalonia," Francesc tells me, matter-of-factly, as he shows me around the beach town, which is graced with opulent 19th century buildings, including the fine Victor Balaguer Museum and Library, appealing squares, a marina, and a lively rambla, and is the site of a once-significant railway and a complex of thriving factories, bombed by Franco's forces during the Spanish Civil War. A bit of local graffiti sums up the fierce clash behind the ongoing political crisis: on a nondescript downtown wall, "Som un nació" ("we are a nation") in Catalan has been scrawled over in black paint with "No somos una nación" ("we are not a nation") in Castilian.

I received, on the first of October, 2017, a brief, cryptic message from an American friend in Paris: "Has the Spanish Civil War broken out all over again?" By coincidence that very morning, I had been working on a chapter of my first novel, set in Barcelona in 1939. I had no notion of what my expat pal was alluding to until I turned on the TV that fall day and watched petrifying footage of police, comandeered by the Madrid government, storming Catalan polling stations, and in some cases, brusquely confiscating ballot boxes, or worse, viciously clubbing people who had come out to vote.

After the Saturday night pyrotechnics and summer hoopla of the Saint John holiday, I sat down with Francesc, on a tranquil Sunday afternoon, to watch footage of the now infamous referendum day: "a referendum that could only be held," as another Catalan writer, Teresa Solana, declares, "thanks to the disciplined complicity of thousands of citizens who combined to fool the Spanish police and secret services. We Catalans had to hide ballot boxes in private houses, in niches in cemeteries, in the bottom of lifts, in the boots of cars, in false ceilings, among the branches of trees . . . And we had to protect our votes with our bodies . . ." Many of the Catalan polling places were located in schools and small villages, and the specter of van-loads of routing police, in glistening, beetle-black uniforms (reminiscent of the sci-fi film *Robocop*), descending on classroom voting places presents a very surreal, sinister, and unsettling picture. The nightmarish physical obstruction of the referendum by the truculent Guardia Civil was halted in the afternoon at the vehement insistence of German chancellor, Angela Merkel. Francesc was at his local polling place, located in the elementary school across from his Barcelona apartment, and as his partner Mireia Sopena (a specialist in Catalan publishing history, with a focus on the first two difficult decades following Franco's victory) mentions, Francesc himself was nearly walloped by police; all in all, a dismal day for sanity and democracy in Europe:

"What have we done," Francesc wonders, "to be thrown back into this abject and intimidating condition of brute political and physical coercion? As a writer, I want to use my language and promote my culture, as a citizen I want a free Catalan republic. Is my vote, and the vote of my neighbours not enough? Are we not equals to other citizens? Why can't I decide my future? Why is someone telling me what I can or can't do? Or say? Or, probably, write? In the election of December 2017, I voted, like millions of Catalans, for legal political parties, and for politicians who are now in prison, or in exile, for a Parliament which has been dissolved and replaced with direct rule from Madrid, due to the absolutism of the Spanish state, following the triggering of article 155 in the Spanish constitution."

The issues surrounding the referendum and recent events in Catalonia are deeply serious, inherently complex, and controversial; not everyone I know in Barcelona was for independence. I have tried, on occasion, to convey to skeptical outsiders unacquainted with Catalan history (who tend to believe most bids for independence are crackpot or extremist) about the longstanding attacks against Catalan culture, including the systematic suppression and public banning, for decades, of the Catalan language— *hable Cristiano* ("speak Christian") Franco's followers demanded, as if prolonging the Spanish Inquisition—and the viciousness of El Caudillo's years in Spain. I can say, from my own experience as a translator and scholar of Catalan literature, that the divisive dynamics that engendered the Spanish Civil War remain abiding and volatile. In 2014, when I taught, for the first time, an honors course called Literary Barcelona, with the aim of highlighting modern and contemporary Catalan literature, at the proposal meeting, I was needled somewhat by a member of my university's Spanish department, I suspect, in order to quell the department's fear that I might be "a Catalan separatist."

In Francesc's own words: "During my life span, I've managed to see the rebirth of a country and a culture that had been viciously crushed after the Spanish Civil War. And now we are back here again, regressed full circle to the same experience of intolerance and brutal arrogance on the part of the Spanish state, which marked my childhood and youth. Despite the familiarity of the state's actions, as a writer—but even more so, as a citizen—I'm unable to comprehend a postulate that denies citizens the equal and democratic right to determine the nature of their political community. *Liberté, égalité, fraternité,* as far as I'm concerned, are not empty, abstracted words; they evoke for me specific values, life-experiences, and memories."

After a lively but productive weekend of fine-tuning *Still Life with Children* one last time, we head back to Barcelona, so Francesc can participate in a radio interview to promote his latest book, *Un estiu* (A Summer), an elegiac and already prize-winning memoir. On the return drive to the city we talk about his sons, whom I got to know on Eivissa (Ibiza) eleven years ago: Pol, who is now working as a financial consultant in London, and Nil, who has just graduated from university.

Parcerisas' latest poem has some of the same rich sonority and allegiance to safeguarding the Catalan language that are hallmarks of the prodigious work of Salvador Espriu, the grand man and high priest of modern Catalan literature, so I coax an obliging Francesc to make a detour to Arenys de Mar, the Costa Maresme town made famous by Espriu as "Sinera." We find a truly disinctive and commendable "art exhibition" in Arenys' famous hilltop cemetery that deftly and elegantly features Espriu-inspired sculptures and intriguing, well-chosen passages of Espriu's poetry. It's a clement and buoyant June day—perfect for an impromptu pilgrimage to the panoramic, cypress-lined cemetery, where the great, indomitable poet (our mutual mentor and tutelary spirit) rests, and the sea-view, the teal blue swatch of the Mediterranean through the arched gate, is stunning.

We're ensconced in Francesc's book-laden apartment in Horta, where 13 years before I listened to him recite his poem, "Objects," and made the quick but firm decision to become his translator. On a sultry summer evening, he asks me to share a recent long poem, "Two Poets Quarreling under the Jacarandas," inspired by incidents in the lives of Salvador Espriu and the Mallorcan poet, Bartomeu Rosselló-Pòrcel, who died at age 24 of tuberculosis (like a Catalan Keats) during the Spanish Civil War. By reading my poem aloud to Francesc and Mireia, I feel as if I'm finally, after over a decade, returning the favor.

While Parcerisas has never been an overtly political poet, the 73-year-old writer has always been dynamically engaged with his beleaguered culture through his impressive verse and the meticulous translation of world literature into his imperiled language: the vital transmission of culture as a form of political advocacy in itself. In the spring of 2018, Francesc had a powerful and memorable opportunity to read in Brussels before members of the exiled Catalan government, so, in closing, I'd like to share a passage from an essay he wrote in English, published recently, in the Welsh magazine, *Planet*, "Follow the Sap Through the Branches: The Role of the Writer after the Catalan Referendum," as well as two of the poems that he recited on that moving occasion in Belgium: "The Shadow," from his last book, *61 Poems*, and a new poem composed in January in the chilling aftermath of the referendum—work that deftly emphasizes the need to preserve and protect Catalan language and culture that for far too long has been under attack:

> We Catalans have an enormous advantage on our side: our language has always been on the sacrificial altar, it has been the language of the once weak and impoverished underdog who fights back. And if we, as poets, can delve into it, we will always be able to make our culture flourish again. As a citizen I will fight for our democratic rights, for civil liberties, for the right to self-determination; as a poet, I will balance words and silence. We cannot take words for granted, and silence can be a rebellion. Let's only speak when searching for truth. . . to be always faithful to our country, our people, our language; to be faithful to our rights. The only tools we can use are words against hate, against terror, against darkness.

L'OMBRA

Sóc l'ombra que segueix l'any,
l'any de la llum o de les falses ombres,
l'any que il·lumina els dies del perdó.
Ara plovisquejava a la boca del metro
i les clofolles eren plenes de silencis,
o plenes de crits. Ha passat la tardor;
la primavera exulta, entre línies,
com la mà maldestre d'un infant
que viu en una llengua que li roben.
No escrivim per salvar-nos,
o per salvar-la. Dia i tenebra dormen
al fons d'una sola mà, d'una sola cosa.
Salva'ns tu, llengua. Salva'ns
o digue'ns com colgar la felicitat
dels noms—i del dolor dels noms—
sota aquesta vinya que era nostra.

The Shadow

I'm the shadow that comes
after the year's close,
a year of light
or of counterfeit shadows—
year that illuminates—
days of forgiveness.
Now there's a light rain
at the metro entrance,
and the shells
are brimming with silences
or rife with screams.
Autumn's over; spring rejoices
in between the lines,
like the clumsy hand of a child
who inhabits a language
someone steals.
We don't write to redeem ourselves
or the language.
Day and darkness rest
in the depth of only one hand,
of only one thing.
Gallant language, it's you
who rescues or reveals
how to bury, beneath this vineyard
that was ours,
the joy—or the agony—of naming.

HEM GUARDAT LES PARAULES...

Hem guardat les paraules per poder dir
llamborda, fossar, congesta.
Per acompanyar l'hivern amb la mimosa,
l'amor amb l'esclat de la rosella.
Hem guardat les paraules per dir tu i jo,
i amorosir l'ells amb el nosaltres.
Per decidir l'encara, la voluntat tossuda
dels rems que trenquen l'aigua,
per restituir la llum a l'alba,
per saber distingir el si del no.
Hem guardat les paraules per als que no hi són.
per als que seran quan no hi siguem,
perquè mai no hi hagi cap presó
i, sense abaixar la veu, puguem dir
olivera, benvingut, mare, llibertat.

gener 2018

To Keep Watch Over Our Language

In order to say
cobblestone, cemetery, glacier,
to pair winter with mimosa,
love with a poppy's burst,
to convey *you* and *I,*
defusing the words *them* and *ours,*
we keep watch over our language.
To go on adopting the stubborn will
of oars breaking the water,
to restore clarity to the dawn,
learning to discern *yes* from *no,*
we safeguard our language,
for those now absent,
for the time when we ourselves
won't be here,
so there will never be a prison
or a muting of our voices
to prevent us from saying
olive tree, welcome, sea, freedom.

January 2018

ABOUT THE AUTHOR

Born in 1944, Francesc Parcerisas, the author of fourteen volumes of poetry, including *Still Life with Children, Triumph of the Present*, and *The Golden Age*, is considered the premier Catalan poet of his generation—a "miracle generation" of poets who came of age as Franco's public banning of the Catalan language came to an end. He is also a masterly, award-winning translator of an impressive array of significant international writers, including T. S. Eliot, F. Scott Fitzgerald, Doris Lessing, Katherine Mansfield, Joyce Carol Oates, Cesare Pavese, Edgar Allan Poe, Ezra Pound, Rimbaud, Susan Sontag, William Styron, and Nobel Laureate Seamus Heaney. Among his numerous translations from French, Italian, and English into Catalan, he is most famous in Catalonia for his translation of Tolkien's *The Lord of the Rings*. His own poems have been translated into Basque, English, French, Gallego, Hungarian, Italian, Portuguese, Slovenian, Spanish, and Welsh, among others.

Among his awards are the 1966 Carles Riba Prize, the 1983 Critics' Prize for Catalan Poetry, the 1983 Catalan Government Prize for Catalan Literature, the 1992 Lletre d'Or Prize for his volume *Triumph of the Present*, the 1992 Serra D'Or Critic's Prize for his Catalan version of Seamus Heaney's *The Haw Lantern*, and the 2001 Cavall Verd-Rafael Jaume Prize for his translation of Ezra Pound's *A Draft of XXX Cantos*. In 2018 the Writers Association awarded him the Premi Jaume Fuster for his contribution to Catalan letters.

From 1998-2005, he was director of the Institute of Catalan Letters in Barcelona. He teaches at the Autonomous University of Barcelona, where he is now Emeritus Professor.

About the Translator

Cyrus Cassells is the author of six books of poetry: *The Mud Actor, Soul Make a Path through Shouting, Beautiful Signor, More Than Peace and Cypresses, The Crossed-Out Swastika*, a finalist for the Balcones Prize for Outstanding Poetry Book of 2012, and *The Gospel according to Wild Indigo*, published in 2018 from Southern Illinois University Press. His first novel, *My Gingerbread Shakespeare*, is forthcoming. His honors include a Lannan Literary Award, a Lambda Literary Award, and the William Carlos Williams Award. He is a Professor of English at Texas State University. His translations of Catalan and Italian poetry have appeared in several anthologies and magazines.

photo by Margo Berdeshevsky

CPSIA information can be obtained
at www.ICGtesting.com
Printed in the USA
FFHW022209310819
54697723-60376FF